A Catholic Confession of Faith

We Believe

Growing Spiritually through the *Catechism of the Catholic Church*

Part One: The Creed

Deacon Henry Libersat

Pauline
BOOKS & MEDIA
Boston

Imprimatur:
† Norbert M. Dorsey, C.P.
Bishop of Orlando
January 22, 1997

Library of Congress Cataloging-in-Publication Data

Libersat, Henry.
  We believe : growing spiritually through the Catechism of the Catholic Church / [Henry Libersat].
    p. cm. — (A Catholic confession of faith)
  ISBN 0-8198-8288-7 (pbk.)
  1. Apostles' Creed. 2. Catholic Church. Catechismus Ecclesiae Catholicae. 3. Catholic Church—Catechisms. I. Title.
II. Series: Libersat, Henry. Catholic confession of faith.
BX1961.5.L43   1997
238'.2—dc21   196-50958
                                                                                 CIP

The Scripture quotations contained herein are from the *New Revised Standard Version Bible: Catholic Edition,* copyright © 1996 and 1989 by the Division of Christian Education of the National Council of Churches of Christ in the U.S.A. Used by permission. All rights reserved.

English translation of the *Catechism of the Catholic Church* for the United States of America copyright © 1994, United States Catholic Conference, Inc.—Libreria Editrice Vaticana. Used with permission.

Copyright © 1997, Henry Libersat

Printed and published in the U.S.A. by Pauline Books & Media, 50 St. Paul's Avenue, Boston, MA 02130.

http://www.pauline.org

E-mail: PBM_EDIT@INTERRAMP.COM

Pauline Books & Media is the publishing house of the Daughters of St. Paul, an international congregation of women religious serving the Church with the communications media.

1 2 3 4   99 98 97

Thanks and Dedication

In a small country cemetery between Henry, Louisiana and Erath, Louisiana, lie the remains of my father and mother, Henry (Sr.) and Elda Libersat. Nearby lie Pierre and Olive, my paternal grandparents. Other relatives are buried there and in another country cemetery in Bancker, Louisiana. Still others lie in Texas and Florida, for example, my maternal grandparents, Clay and Cora Zeringue.

These relatives have been a great part of my life, even since their death. They all loved me and cared for me in so many different ways. They were all Catholic and lived the faith as best they could, given their understanding of it. They all knew and loved God.

I want to dedicate *A Catholic Confession of Faith,* to them all. This "work" is actually four small books, *We Believe, We Celebrate the Mystery, We Live the Good Life,* and *We Pray.*

But in a very special way, these four books are dedicated to the memory of my wonderful parents, whose love for God and the Church gave me the foundation for my life as husband, father and grandfather, as well as for my recent decade of ministry in the Catholic Church as a deacon and for my nearly four decades of service in the Catholic press.

Thanks, Mom. Thanks, Dad.

Thanks, too, to those many priests, sisters and faithful laity whose example, love and encouragement have kept me trying to live the good life.

Truly, I am grateful to the bishop-publishers of *The Florida Catholic* for the opportunity to serve God and the Church through that interdiocesan publishing venture. I am grateful for their trust and pastoral guidance.

I am also grateful to the Daughters of St. Paul for their confidence in me and for their encouragement in my extra-curricular writing. This series brings to six the number of books I have written for Pauline Books & Media. The first two, *Way, Truth and Life* and *Do Whatever He Tells You* are presentations of our Catholic faith from a perspective of daily life. They are rooted in doctrine, Scripture and prayer, but are written in a more popular style. While I have tried to use real-life stories in this series, the books here are a bit more formal in presentation and more directly concerned with Church teaching as presented in the *Catechism of the Catholic Church*.

Given the reader response to the material as it was presented in *The Florida Catholic*, I have high hopes that these books will help many more readers. In series form in the newspaper, the material was used by many people in religious education, Re-Membering Church and RCIA, as well as for personal reflection.

Contents

CHAPTER 1
How Do We Know God Exists? 17

CHAPTER 2
Three Persons in One God 21

CHAPTER 3
The Father Almighty, Creator of Heaven and Earth 25

CHAPTER 4
And in Jesus Christ, His Only Son, Our Lord 29

CHAPTER 5
Who Was Conceived by the Holy Spirit,
Born of the Virgin Mary 35

CHAPTER 6
Suffered under Pontius Pilate, Was Crucified,
Died and Was Buried. He Descended into Hell 39

CHAPTER 7
On the Third Day, He Arose Again from the Dead 43

CHAPTER 8
He Ascended into Heaven
and Is Seated at the Right Hand of the Father 47

CHAPTER 9
From Thence He Will Come to Judge
the Living and the Dead 51

CHAPTER 10
I Believe in the Holy Spirit 55

CHAPTER 11
The Holy Catholic Church 59

CHAPTER 12
The Holy Catholic Church... *(continued)* 63

CHAPTER 13
The Communion of Saints 67

CHAPTER 14
The Forgiveness of Sins 71

CHAPTER 15
The Resurrection of the Body 77

CHAPTER 16
And Life Everlasting 81

CHAPTER 17
Amen! 87

About *A Catholic Confession of Faith*...

I thought I was "riding high" when Pauline Books & Media agreed to print a revision of two series of articles in book form. *We Believe* and *We Celebrate the Mystery* had already been published in *The Florida Catholic*. I had done what I started out to do. Honestly, I thought I was "written out" for at least another few months.

When Sister Mary Mark of Pauline Books & Media mentioned yet two more books, one on morality and one on prayer, I inwardly gulped but immediately said, "Yes, I will be happy to do them!" I gulped because I realized the amount of work I was taking on. But I immediately agreed to do the two other books for three good reasons.

First, it was a good idea and one I would share first of all with readers of *The Florida Catholic*. This statewide Catholic newspaper is my first professional love. Second, it seemed the Holy Spirit was talking to the Sisters: *We Believe* shared the content of our faith; *We Celebrate the Mystery* spoke of the awesome and loving presence of God in our sacramental life. Now, *We Live the Good Life* will help people refocus on how we respond to God's great love, and *We Pray* will discuss the wonderful ways God invites us into a personal relationship with him. Third, I realized I must personally revisit my own response to God's love, and the *Catechism of the Catholic Church* would be a wonderful aid in this task. Doing the books would make me do what I needed to do.

Each chapter in these four books ends with a reflection which will hopefully help individuals and groups to think about and discuss the material presented.

It is my prayer that all readers will benefit in reading *A Catholic Confession of Faith* as I did in writing them. The work was a joy; the response to the work was a blessing. May it give glory to God who is Father, Son and Spirit!

> Deacon Henry Libersat
> Pentecost, 1996

We Believe...
About This Book...

A bishop commented, "We've lost two generations of Catholics. They don't know what to believe; they don't know what the Church teaches."

Truth has a liberating power. This little book, and the other three books in *A Catholic Confession of Faith,* invite Catholics and others to reflect on some of the basic beliefs of the Catholic Church, and to do so only for the sake of encountering and embracing truth as revealed by God.

In recent decades, truth has been approached rather subjectively and pragmatically. For example, God's demand for justice has been equated too often with secular, political, legal and economic movements. Or justice has been recommended only through emotional appeal: "See how these poor children have distended bellies? Don't you feel sorry for them? Won't you help them? After all, they, too, are children of God."

While rooted in truth, this appeal to just action is rather shallow. It ignores the fact that justice is not so much action as it is a way of life. Just as faith is not only faithfulness to Sunday Mass, so justice is not only good works. Justice is the ultimate expression of faith and love. Justice is part of who God is, so true biblical justice finds root in the very heart of God. Christians learn to live a just life through communion with God.

Mother Teresa puts it this way:

> The fruit of silence is prayer;
> The fruit of prayer is faith;
> The fruit of faith is love;
> The fruit of love is service;
> The fruit of service of justice;
> The fruit of justice is peace.

The purpose of this book is to help people reflect on the truths of our faith—those truths which are given us by God through both Scripture and Tradition. They are considered here objectively, as valuable in themselves, apart from any pragmatic considerations. Objective truth is where we begin, for it is God's revelation of both his heart and will.

I have chosen the Apostles' Creed as the foundation of this reflection. It contains the fundamental elements of the faith of all Christians and of us Catholics in a special way, embracing both sources of divine revelation: Scripture and Tradition. When we recite the Creed, it is from a different historical and traditional perspective than that of other Christians, even though we all profess faith in Jesus Christ as Son of God.

At the end of each brief chapter, readers will find a "Reflection" which may be of help in thinking about or discussing our faith.

Where possible I have used examples from everyday family life, including the entertainment industry, to help us relate to the objective truths which, are so often misunderstood by so many people. Truth so often seems "beyond" our comprehension and even experience. However, it is my belief that it's the very "beyond–us–ness" of the mystery of revealed truth that makes it both enticing and believable. The human heart and mind love truth. Truth revealed in mystery appeals both to our imagination and to that innate desire to see above and beyond ourselves, to touch, however briefly and inadequately, the Beginning and the End from whom we come and to whom we are going.

> Deacon Henry Libersat
> Easter, 1995

CHAPTER 1

How Do We Know God Exists?

The college student glared at the older man and declared, "I don't believe in God. I'm an atheist. If there is a God, prove it to me."

For the first time, this Catholic layman had been challenged to defend his belief in God. "How do I do this?" he thought. "I've explained my Catholic faith to others who already believe in God, but how do I explain belief in God to an atheist?" That's a good question. Older Catholics recall that "faith is a gift from God." As Catholics, we believe that through faith we know God personally as Creator, Savior and Advocate. But putting faith aside for just a moment, by human reason we can establish the fact that God exists.

• Logic leads us to believe that there must be a God, an uncreated source for all other things. The source has to be entirely Other than anything created. The source or Creator must be completely self-sufficient, without beginning or end.

• The Creator has to have intelligence—just look at the order of creation, the universe and our own planet Earth.

• The beauty of nature speaks of a beautiful source. Who can look at a sunrise or sunset, falling snow, rain forests, mountains and plains, rivers and oceans, birds and butterflies, jet planes and ocean liners and not see in and behind them all a beautiful Creator?

- A marvelous relationship exists among all created things, with each species somehow relying on other plant and animal species for life. In humans, that relationship rises to a higher spiritual plane when people love and serve one another, care for creation and provide for the common good. Creation is only a faint representation (or symbol) of the wondrous and surpassing relationship that exists in God.
- Creation is fruitful. Each species reproduces itself. Plants beget plants; animals beget animals; humans beget humans. The Creator is fruitful; the natural order of creation proves that. For believers, the order of grace shows an even more beautiful fruitfulness in God.
- In creation, most notably in humans, we find the power to communicate. Speech, the written word, radio, television, cinema and computer networks are examples of how humans communicate. Other creatures communicate as well. Animals can call to one another announcing food, danger, fear, loneliness or the desire to mate.

The Creator has also communicated existence—life itself, intelligence, and for human beings, the invitation to eternal life.

Humans enjoy a special kind of communication—love for one another. Men and women form lasting relationships; fathers and mothers love their children. This generates a sense of belonging, of needing to know one another. Parents want their children to know who they are. Can it be the same with God? If we have a desire to know and be known by others, is it not possible, even probable, that the Creator desires to reveal himself more clearly to us, his children?

Here is where faith comes in. Knowledge about God and belief in God are not the same thing. A person could be a scholar and know very much about God but still be a non-believer. By reason we can know something about God. But we learn many more things through revelation, that is, God speaking to us through the prophets and all of Scripture, especially through his divine Son incarnate in Jesus Christ. The *Catechism of the Catholic Church* observes: "Man is by nature and vocation a religious being. Coming from God, going toward God, man lives a fully human life only if he freely lives by his bond with God" (no. 44). "Without the Creator, the creature vanishes" *(Gaudium et Spes,* no. 36). "This is the reason why believers know that the love of Christ urges them to bring the light of the living God to those who do not know him or who reject him" (no. 49).

We can never know everything about God because God is infinite. By reason, however, we can be predisposed for the gift of faith, since faith is not opposed to reason (cf. *Catechism,* no. 35). Seeing manifestations of God, we are drawn to know God more perfectly. Faith is the acceptance of God in his profound mystery. Faith is expressed by obedience and worship and conformity to the will of God.

In faith, we know that God has indeed revealed himself. He has given us his name:

"I Am Who Am!"

He tells us about his relationship with us:

"I will be your God and you will be my people!"

He gives us the keys to fullness of life:

"I am the Lord your God; you will not have strange gods before me; remember to keep holy the sabbath day; you shall not kill, steal, commit adultery, covet...."

In faith, we know that God has revealed himself as

Father, Son and Holy Spirit. That is the mysterious relationship which creates and sustains all creation from angel to ameba to atom.

Reflection:

- Have you ever looked on the beauties of nature and felt close to God?
- At what point in your life did you want to *know God* rather than only know *about* him? Share these thoughts with a friend.

Chapter 2

Three Persons in One God

The late Frank Sheed was a prominent lecturer, author and lay theologian. Many years ago I had the pleasure and honor to hear and interview him. As a leader of the Catholic Evidence Guild in London, he lived and preached the Catholic faith tirelessly. He used to do "street-corner preaching," standing on boxes to tell people about our God and Church.

Mr. Sheed often said that the best way to capture a crowd was to speak about two great truths—the Holy Trinity and the Real Presence of Jesus in the Eucharist. These powerful mysteries stopped hecklers more than once, the lay preacher said. (Happily, some of Mr. Sheed's books are being reprinted today. Among the best for readers just beginning to look into theology are *Theology for Beginners* and *Theology and Sanity.*)

For centuries Christians have pondered the mystery of the Trinity. A legend about the great intellectual St. Augustine says that one day he was walking along the beach and he saw a young boy with a small bucket. The boy was taking water from the sea and pouring it into a small hole he had dug in the sand. The boy poured bucket after bucket of water into that tiny opening in the sand.

Augustine asked, "What are you doing?"

"I'm putting the sea into this small hole," the boy replied.

The saint chuckled. "You can't do that," he said. "The sea is too big for that little hole."

The boy looked at St. Augustine and said, "And God is too big for your small mind." Then the boy disappeared.

The story is a legend, but it makes a strong point. God is too big for our small minds. We can never hope to understand how God "always was and always will be," and how he has "no beginning and no end." Much less can we hope to understand how God is three divine Persons in one God. But that's how God through Jesus Christ has revealed himself—as one God who is at once Father, Son and Holy Spirit, three distinct Persons each fully possessing the one divine nature.

Cardinal John Henry Newman, that saintly great intellectual who converted to Catholicism from the Anglican Church, once said that "a thousand difficulties do not make one doubt." It is impossible to fully understand the Trinity, but faith enables us to accept the mystery. I cannot understand how the sun, which is all gas according to science, does not just finally burn itself out. But my lack of understanding does not dim the brilliance of the sun or lessen its heat.

The mystery of the Holy Trinity (three divine Persons each equally possessing the one divine nature) can never be fully understood. The Trinity cannot be put under a microscope, dissected and analyzed. However, if we want to embrace more fully our God—the Father and the Son and the Holy Spirit—we must try to appreciate what the Church teaches about the Trinity.

Briefly, each Person (Father, Son and Spirit) is wholly and completely God. There is one God. The Persons do not share the divine nature among themselves;

they each fully possess it. They are one—the Father is wholly in the Son; the Son is wholly in the Father and the Spirit is wholly in both. They are one divine nature but three distinct divine Persons.

Everything has being from the Father, through the Son and in the Holy Spirit. The Father generates the Son; the Son is begotten and the Spirit proceeds from them both (cf. *Catechism*, nos. 249-260). However, these "activities" are not done in a sequence of time. The relationship is present without beginning or end in the very nature of God who is. He named himself: "I Am Who Am."

Now, isn't that perfectly clear? Of course not, but it will be helpful to pray to God as Trinity, to pay attention when we bless ourselves or others with the sign of the cross. It will be helpful to study the *Catechism's* treatment of the Holy Trinity, asking God to help us accept with joy and gratitude this great mystery which he has revealed to us, his children.

Reflection:

- Does the mystery of three Persons in one God challenge or comfort you? Why?

- Find a quiet place. Sit in silence and prayerfully place yourself in God's presence. Ask God to help you embrace fully the divine reality of the Most Holy Trinity. Imagine God drawing you into himself. Lose yourself in God.

- After you've done this, thank God for whatever happened. Maybe you "felt" his presence; maybe you were only bored or nervous. That's okay. Thank God, for he is always with you, knows you and loves you.

Chapter 3

The Father Almighty, Creator of Heaven and Earth...

A young Catholic was having trouble relating to God as Father. His experience of "father" had been wanting, since he and his natural father did not get on well and did not understand each other. His spiritual director told him: "Focus on Jesus Christ. One day you'll wake up and realize you know the Father."

Jesus brings us to the Father through the Holy Spirit. We cannot relate to Jesus without relating to Abba, his loving Father, for whom he laid down his life, or to the Spirit under whose overshadowing he was conceived. Our God is a Holy Trinity.

How is God our Father? Most obviously, in the order of creation, he is Father because he gave us being, gave us life and supplied us with all we need to live. But he is not a distant God. He is not an absentee Father. He has come with Jesus and the Spirit to live in us. The Spirit is the gift of Jesus and the Father. The Father already loves us, protects us and has given us to Jesus (cf. Jn 14:16, 26; 15:26, 16:27, 17:11, 24).

Our faith tells us that God so loved us that he sent his only Son to become man, to die in our place, to close the chasm between us and God (cf. Jn 3:16). That chasm was created by the sin of our first parents. The Son of God assumed to himself a human nature. He became a specific man, Jesus of Nazareth, the Christ, the Savior. In his time on earth, Jesus taught us that God is a loving Father. The Father proved his love for us through his most perfect gift, his Son who became a man while remaining God. (Later we will reflect on Jesus as both God and man.)

Jesus said that in seeing him, we see the Father (cf. Jn 14:8-10). Jesus is the perfect revelation of the Father, far above the rest of revelation through the prophets. As the perfect revelation of the Father, Jesus healed the sick, fed the hungry, forgave sinners (even those who put him to death), raised the dead, and promised everlasting life to those who accept him as Lord.

In and through Jesus, we have met the Father—and Jesus reveals the Father as kind, compassionate, loving, long-suffering. We know this is true because that's the way Jesus is. How else could it be, since the Son is in the Father and the Father is in the Son—since they, with the Spirit, are one God? In John's Gospel, Jesus tells us, "The Father and I are one" and "I have shown you many good works from the Father" (Jn 10:30, 32). Jesus gave us his Father. He tells us clearly, "I am ascending to my Father and your Father, to my God and your God" (Jn 20:17).

How can we come to know the Father better? First of all, by drawing closer to Jesus. Spending time gazing at a crucifix is a good way to get to know God the Father. The Father loves us so much he sent his Son to die for us. Read the Gospels prayerfully. Reflect on how Jesus loved the Father, how he went off alone to be with his Father in prayer. Remember that God is our Father, too, and he will not refuse us when we ask to draw closer to him. To better understand Scripture, read carefully the introductions to the various books in the Bible, the footnotes and the cross references.

Reflection:

- Have you ever found it hard to relate to God as a loving Father? Why?
- How can you grow in your relationship with the Father?
- In a quiet place, meditate on Jesus who is the perfect image of the Father. Jesus told Philip: "When you've seen me, you've seen the Father" (cf. Jn 14:9).

CHAPTER 4

And in Jesus Christ, His Only Son, Our Lord...

It's a standard joke in most families, especially around Christmas time: "When everything else fails, read the instructions!" Those "easy-to-assemble" toys aren't so easy to assemble after all. You can't just make things go your own way. You don't put the tricycle's one big wheel on the back axle. If you do, you'll have a rather strange contraption that won't go anywhere.

The same principle applies in our spiritual life. We are put together by God. We are taught by God. He reveals himself to us, especially in Jesus Christ, God's only begotten Son and our Lord.

Jesus is the Son of God. He had no earthly Father, but he was conceived by the power of the Holy Spirit. The beautiful story from Luke's Gospel about the birth of Jesus is familiar to most people. The angel came to Mary and told her she was to be the mother of God's Son. She agreed. The Holy Spirit overshadowed her and she conceived a baby who was both God and man. She and Joseph were to give him the name of Jesus because *he will save his people from their sins* (cf. Mt 1:21; Lk 1:31ff.).

It is hard for some people to believe that Jesus had no human father. But God is God, and nothing is impossible to him. No truly Christian church has ever claimed that

Jesus had a human father. We believe that Jesus was both God and man.

We believe, too, that Mary was a virgin. The conception of Jesus in her womb fulfilled the prophesies from Isaiah that a virgin would conceive and bear a Son who was to be Messiah and Savior. Catholics believe that Mary had no other children—that she was always a virgin, before and after the birth of Jesus. This authoritative teaching of the Church is difficult to understand but must be accepted in faith. The Church can teach no error in matters of faith and morals because Jesus promised to protect his Church.

When we think of Jesus of Nazareth, it is important to remember that there are three Persons in the Blessed Trinity and that Jesus is the Second Person of the Trinity made man. A divine Person, he has both a divine nature and a human nature. At his name both heaven and earth bow and confess his lordship (cf. Phil 2:9-10).

Christ as *God*-Man

Christ, as *God*-man, is Lord. All things are under his dominion. God the Son was human as Jesus of Nazareth. God the Son is divine because he is the Second Person of the Blessed Trinity, who possesses the one divine nature with the Father and the Holy Spirit. As a divine Person, he is the only Son of God. In *Theology for Beginners,* the renowned lay theologian Frank Sheed explained Jesus this way: the Second Person of the Blessed Trinity, who is God the Son, assumed human nature unto himself. At the moment of conception, God the Son was fully God and fully human.

The early Christians suffered estrangement from their Jewish families and friends because they proclaimed Jesus as Lord. He was divine as well as human. Accepting

Jesus as Lord was a revolutionary religion, a life-changing (even life-threatening) faith. Jesus himself said that faith in him would divide parents and children, husbands and wives (cf. Mt 10:35ff.).

To say that Jesus is Lord is to say that he has dominion over all things and that every allegiance is owed him. If Christians truly accept Jesus as Lord, they obey the commandments of God and the teachings of the Church. Otherwise their lives, like the mis-assembled tricycle, run rather lopsided and helter-skelter.

What can it mean to us to accept Jesus as Lord? First, it means we set aside false gods—idols in which we take refuge—such as wealth, comfort, security, superstition, power and popularity. We live more for others. We see each person as an image of God, someone loved by God. We work hard for peace in the home, on the job, in schools and in all relationships. If Jesus is our Lord, we take seriously his call to meet the needs of others. We see ourselves as modern day Good Samaritans who are willing to go out of our way to help others.

If Jesus is our Lord, we do all these things because they are what Jesus did or said to do. In the letter of James, we learn: "What good is it, my brothers and sisters, if you say you have faith but do not have works? Can faith save you?... So faith by itself, if it has no works, is dead. But someone will say, 'You have faith and I have works.' Show me your faith apart from your works, and I by my works will show you my faith" (Jas 2:14, 17-18).

Second, if Jesus is Lord, we follow him as the "way, and the truth, and the life" (Jn 14:6a). Our complete trust is in him because he is the way of love directly into the heart of the Father. "No one comes to the Father except through me" (Jn 14:6b). We accept his authority and the authority of the Church he founded. We believe—as we pray in the Apostles' Creed—in the one, holy, catholic and apostolic Church. We embrace the teachings of the Church and accept and respect the role of the Holy Father and the bishops as successors of Peter and the other apostles.

To say "Jesus is Lord" without surrendering to him is to miss the point of his lordship and the wonderful opportunity to find true freedom by obedience to God. As Pope John Paul II teaches in his encyclical on moral theology, *Splendor of Truth*, true freedom is found only in becoming what God intends us to become, by obeying God, who is the author of life and the beginning and the end of our existence.

Christ as God-*Man*

Christ as God-*man* understands us. We take great joy in our Savior who is both God and man. As a human being, Jesus "grew and became strong, filled with wisdom; and the favor of God was upon him" (Lk 2:40). Jesus had to learn to walk and to talk, even to pray. He knew human suffering and joy, and he even experienced temptation. In Jesus, we know that God has felt what we feel. He is approachable and knowable. We know that he understands us.

"For we do not have a high priest who is unable to sympathize with our weaknesses, but we have one who in every respect has been tested as we are, yet without sin" (Heb 4:15, cf. Jn 8:46, Rom 8:3, 2 Cor 5:21). To believe in Jesus, who is both God and man, is to embrace him as the way, truth and life (Jn 14:6).

Reflection:

- Have you ever felt like a mis-assembled tricycle? If so, what caused this feeling? How did you cope with it?
- Do you truly believe that Jesus is at once fully God and fully man?
- Meditate on the Incarnation and birth of Jesus in Luke 1:26-2:14. Ask God to help you believe and love the mystery of Jesus, true God and true man.

CHAPTER 5

Who Was Conceived by the Holy Spirit, Born of the Virgin Mary...

As a deacon I treasure the experience of baptizing babies. Whether they sleep or wail throughout the ceremony, it is beautiful and precious to see proud parents come to the Church to give their children to God.

I remember one baptism in particular. The mother was unwed. She was accompanied by her parents and other members of her family. She seemed a little embarrassed about having a baby out of wedlock, but her faith and family gave her courage to get on with life, to do her best to rear her child according to her faith.

Two thousand years ago Mary's faith was tested in a similar but infinitely different way. In those days, according to Jewish law, bearing a child out of wedlock was punishable by being stoned to death. Mary was invited by God to conceive a child without a human father. Mary had to worry about whether Joseph would understand and if he did not, what would happen to her. When she said *yes* to God, she put herself entirely in God's hands. She trusted God. Joseph, who knew Mary so well, was doubtful until an angel told him to marry her, that her child was indeed the Son of God (cf. Mt 1:20).

Mary was a virgin. The prophets had said that the Messiah would be born of a virgin, and that Bethlehem, the town of David, would be the birthplace of the Messiah.

That Mary was a virgin and ever remained a virgin is a matter of doctrine in the Catholic Church. We believe, in faith, that Mary conceived by the power of the Holy Spirit, as Luke's Gospel relates in that beautiful nativity narrative proclaimed every Christmas. The *Catechism of the Catholic Church* explains: "In Mary, the Holy Spirit *fulfills* the plan of the Father's loving goodness. With and through the Holy Spirit, the Virgin conceives and gives birth to the Son of God. By the Holy Spirit's power and her faith, her virginity became uniquely fruitful" (no. 723). We believe, in faith, that Jesus, the Son of God, is at once both God and man.

Adam and Eve were created sinless, but they chose to sin. Jesus was never touched by sin, not even original sin. While he was in Mary's womb he was in a pure temple, unstained by sin.

Our faith tells us that Mary was never tainted by sin, not even original sin. That's what we mean by the Immaculate Conception of Mary. The Church teaches that this occurred through the "foreseen merits of Jesus Christ." Because God is not limited by time, God applied the future merits of Jesus' saving death to Mary at the moment she was conceived in her mother's womb.

"But how can this be?" some may ask. "How can God do that *before* Jesus died for us?" God is not limited by time. He accepts the Savior's death for the salvation of all those who lived before Christ and all those who have lived at Christ's time and since, including you and me. It was entirely within God's infinite power to apply the foreseen merits of Christ's death for Mary in a unique way—that is, to preserve her from original sin.

Through Jesus, we too are children of God and of Mary. St. Pacian, a fourth century Spanish bishop, said that through baptism by a priest, while faith presides over the ceremony, the Holy Spirit brings forth a new person nourished in the womb of his or her mother, the Church *(Office of Readings,* Friday of the 19th week of ordinary time).

We, too, are children of God. The same Spirit that overshadowed the womb of Mary overshadows the "womb" of the Church, the baptismal font, and we are born into new life, the very life of God. The *Catechism* teaches: "The fruit of Baptism, or baptismal grace, is a rich reality that includes forgiveness of original sin and all personal sins, birth into the new life by which man becomes an adoptive son of the Father, a member of Christ and a temple of the Holy Spirit. By this very fact the person baptized is incorporated into the Church, the Body of Christ, and made a sharer in the priesthood of Christ" (no. 1279).

We are also children of Mary because we are members of Christ's Body, of which she is mother. As he hung from the cross, Jesus gave Mary to us as our mother through John: "Woman, here is your son.... Here is your mother" (Jn 19:26-27). She is mother of the Son of God and of the adoptive sons and daughters of God.

Reflection:

- You are born again of the same Holy Spirit who overshadowed Mary. Through Jesus, you are a child of God and you share in God's divine life. Reflect on this beautiful truth.
- How can I thank God for the gift of adoption?
- Do I embrace Mary as my mother, since she is mother of Jesus, who is my Brother as well as my God and Savior?

Chapter 6

Suffered under Pontius Pilate, Was Crucified, Died and Was Buried. He Descended into Hell...

On Good Friday, 1981, the narrow streets of old Jerusalem teemed with people from all parts of the world. They walked somberly on the way to Calvary. Remarkably, the local people in Jerusalem went about business as usual. Stores were open. Merchants hawked their wares, calling out to pilgrims on the Way of the Cross, offering discounts on already reduced merchandise.

One man was leaning against a storefront. As an attractive young woman walked by him, absorbed in her prayers, he made a remark that in polite terms would be called harassment. And so the scene played: faith and devotion in the midst of business as usual.

It was probably like that on the first Good Friday. When Jesus carried his cross, shops were open and people were running about their business. Even his closest friends had deserted him. Only his mother, a young man and two other women would remain with him to the bitter end. The people for whom Jesus was dying did not know him. They ridiculed him and cast curious noncommittal glances at this condemned prisoner, already weak from torture and hovering on the brink of death.

Jesus did suffer under Pontius Pilate. The victim of hatred, Jesus had angered Jewish leaders. They in turn had presented him to Pilate as an enemy of the emperor. Pilate, afraid for his position in the Roman Empire, had succumbed to the hateful demands of the crowd and condemned Jesus to death. But first, Jesus was scourged and mocked and crowned with thorns.

Jesus did die. He was nailed to a cross. With the nails piercing his hands and feet, the cross was raised and dropped into the hole prepared for it. His body jerked against the nails. He hung suspended between heaven and earth, condemned as a criminal, but truly the Son of God, truly the Savior of the world.

Many people have preached and written about the death of Jesus. He gave up his right to justice and chose to die in our place. He was innocent, without sin or guilt, the unblemished Lamb of God, the perfect sacrifice, both victim and priest, offering himself in sacrifice for sinful humanity.

Although he had legions of angels at his disposal, he walked the way of the cross alone. Under the fierce Palestinian sun, he hung for three hours on the cross, suffering excruciating pain until at last he suffocated. Things he said on the cross echo in the human heart: "Father, forgive them; for they do not know what they are doing" (Lk 23:34).

"Forgive them." He even made an excuse for us. "They don't know what they are doing." We have heard so often that Jesus, the Word of God, the Son of God, is the "perfect revelation of the Father." No scripture passage, no gospel story, no pious thought or description of God can say "God the Father" as well as Jesus does by who he is and what he does. The Father whom Jesus shows us is a God willing to give his Son over to death so we can live. Such love surpasses understanding.

Jesus suffered and he died. He said something rather strange on the cross before he died: "It is finished." Satan is not the victor! Jesus, the Son of God, is the true victor! "It is finished. Now, Father, that I have given all I have to give, the victory is won, humanity is redeemed, the gates of heaven are opened, the powers of hell are defeated and death itself has lost all its sting." As the *Catechism of the Catholic Church* explains (no. 272): "Christ crucified is thus 'the power of God and the wisdom of God. For the foolishness of God is wiser than men, and the weakness of God is stronger than men' (1 Cor 1:24-25). It is in Christ's resurrection and exaltation that the Father has shown forth 'the immeasurable greatness of his power in us who believe' (Eph 1:19-22)."

The *Catechism* holds: *"Death is transformed by Christ.* Jesus, the Son of God, also himself suffered the death that is part of the human condition. Yet, despite his anguish as he faced death, he accepted it in an act of complete and free submission to his Father's will. The obedience of Jesus has transformed the curse of death into a blessing" (no. 1009).

The *Catechism* teaches that "Christian death has a positive meaning" (no. 1010). St. Paul, who lived completely for Christ, saw death as the ultimate blessing, the final leap into the arms of Jesus. He said, "For to me, living is Christ and dying is gain" (Phil 1:21). The *Catechism* continues, "What is essentially new about Christian death is this: through Baptism, the Christian has already 'died with Christ' sacramentally, in order to live a new life; and if we die in Christ's grace, physical death completes this 'dying with Christ' and so completes our incorporation into him in his redeeming act."

What humiliation for Satan! The devil's most powerful and wicked plan has backfired. Already, Satan knows that the tomb will be empty in three days. Already he sees the army of white-robed saints and martyrs in heaven.

Satan's victory was his defeat. Obedience to the Father was the power that upset evil and dissipated darkness. Obedience to God's will, even to the death, was the key to freedom which Jesus gave each and every one of us. In surrendering to God, we become victors. In embracing God's will, we discover true freedom.

Jesus was set free from death, from the grave. They had put him in a tomb and rolled a big stone over the entrance. But a stone, no matter how large, cannot contain God. As the old spiritual tells it, "The angels rolled the stone away."

Now we have an empty tomb, a risen Lord and a wonderful road to travel with Jesus the Lord.

Reflection:

- Jesus was truly a man. He suffered great physical and emotional pain during his passion and death. Consider yourself in his place: you are innocent but found guilty; you came with love but you are hated; you forgive, but people condemn you. How do you respond to such treatment?

- Visit a cemetery. Read the tombstones and reflect on how fast life goes by. What is really important in your life? What are the most precious gifts you will leave behind? What will you take with you on your way home to God?

- Prayerfully reflect on the crucified Jesus and on his love for you.

CHAPTER 7

On the Third Day, He Arose Again from the Dead...

The movie *ET* stole the heart of America. Isn't it strange that such an unusual creature made so great an impression on people of all ages? Children and the elderly identified with the story about this being who came from the heavens.

The story appealed to people because it spoke to their sense of transcendence. ET was something beyond us, yet still with us. He brought out the best in good people and the worst in bad people. He came from above and returned to the heavens—but only after he had been misunderstood, imprisoned and abused, only after he had died and come back to life.

Doesn't that sound familiar? ET is a messianic figure. His story, in fairy-tale form, is like the story of Jesus Christ, the Son of God, who came from heaven to earth, walked among us, taught us, performed great works, was loved and hated, imprisoned, died, rose from the dead and ascended into heaven.

ET appeals to us because the movie capitalizes on our own sense of immortality, which was given us at creation. We are made in the image of God; therefore we are destined to live forever. Even death does not snuff us out. We will live forever in eternal happiness or sadness. At the end of the movie, ET tells his young earthling friend not to cry because he is going back into the heavens. He tells the boy that he will always be with him "right here," touching the boy's chest, over his heart. That rings of Jesus' promise to his disciples, "I am with you always, to the end of the age" and "Where two or three are gathered in my name, I am there among them" (Mt 28:20 and Mt 18:20).

ET evoked a sort of spiritual nostalgia in people. The resurrection of Jesus should evoke a lively hope and a joyful sense of gratitude. For the resurrection of Jesus is the promise of our own resurrection from the dead, of our own eternal life in God.

After his resurrection, Jesus did not appear to the town crier, high priest or government officials of his day. As the *Catechism of the Catholic Church* and the Scriptures remind us, he appeared to his disciples, to those who had been with him and had come with him from Galilee to Jerusalem (cf. Acts 13:31, Jn 14:22, *Catechism,* no. 647). We might wonder why Jesus appeared only to those who had followed him. Why not prove his resurrection to Pilate, to those who had scourged him, to those who had nailed him to the cross?

The *Catechism* tells us it was because his resurrection is far more valuable than merely historical data. His resurrection is the keystone of apostolic faith. St. Paul himself said that if Christ were not raised from the dead, our faith would be worthless (cf. 1 Cor 15:17). The apostles and disciples needed the resurrection to understand who Jesus really was and to know that all his teachings and promises were from God. The resurrection is the fuel of faith.

The *Catechism* teaches: "The resurrection above all constitutes the confirmation of all Christ's works and teachings. All truths, even those most inaccessible to human reason, find their justification if Christ by his resurrection has given the definitive proof of his divine authority, which he had promised" (no. 651).

The resurrection does confirm Jesus' divinity. He had said, "When you have lifted up the Son of Man, then you will realize that I am he" (Jn 8:28). From the *Catechism*: "The resurrection of the crucified one shows that he was truly 'I Am,' the Son of God and God himself" (no. 653).

Since he had risen from the dead—and following the coming of the Holy Spirit—the infant Church would preach the resurrection of Christ with conviction and power. So powerful was the faith of the apostles and other disciples that thousands upon thousands were converted to the Christian faith.

Peter's first sermon on Pentecost (cf. Acts 2:14ff.) was based on the resurrection of Jesus whom the people had crucified. Jesus, risen from the dead, is the promised Messiah. The marvel of the resurrection fired the souls of the believers. Jesus was risen, alive, ascended into heaven. His Holy Spirit was with the Church until the time when Jesus would come again.

ET, that lovable little character, cannot promise us our own resurrection. Jesus can and does. The resurrection of Christ, according to the *Catechism* (no. 655), "is the principle and source of our future resurrection: 'Christ has been raised from the dead, the first fruits of those who have fallen asleep.... For as in Adam all die, so also in Christ shall all be made alive.' The risen Christ lives in the hearts of his faithful while they await that fulfillment. In Christ, Christians 'have tasted...the powers of the age to come' (Heb 6:5) and their lives are swept up by Christ into the heart of divine life, so that they may 'live no longer for themselves but for him who for their sake died and was raised' (2 Cor 5:15, cf. Col 3:1-3)."

Reflection:

- Am I touched deeply by the resurrection of Jesus? Is this real for me?
- *ET* gives a spiritual message. Think about how it parallels the story of Jesus' passion, death and resurrection. Why do some people embrace ET still and remain unmoved by Jesus?
- Pray for renewed and fervent faith among all Christians.

Chapter 8

He Ascended into Heaven and Is Seated at the Right Hand of the Father...

A story is told about a dying cardinal who had a vision on his deathbed. He told his surrounding confreres that he saw God the Father seated on his throne in heaven. His glory shone brightly while around him all the angels and archangels were basking in God's love and singing his praises. Joy, peace and love filled the whole scene.

Suddenly, God the Father looked up as his eyes fastened on something in the distance. Slowly a great smile spread across his face. A figure of a solitary man appeared in the distance. As he walked toward God's throne, he too began to smile and walked even faster. The Father himself rose from his throne and walked down the golden steps. While the man in the distance broke into a fast trot, the Father moved away from the throne and hurried toward him.

Seeing the Father coming toward him, the man began to run as fast as he could toward the Father. He began to laugh and shout: "Father! Father!" God the Father himself began to run and shouted: "Jesus! Jesus!" At last God the Father and Jesus met. They embraced tightly, each laughing and calling the other's name: "Father!" "Jesus!"

Whether or not this story is true, the message it gives us is most definitely true. Jesus ascended into heaven after he rose from the dead. He is with the Father in heaven, seated in the highest place of honor, at the Father's right hand. The *Catechism of the Catholic Church* tells us that "sitting at God's right hand" means that Jesus Christ the man as well as the Second Person of the Holy Trinity is now "seated bodily after he became incarnate and his flesh was glorified" (no. 663).

The story of the cardinal's vision awakens in us a deep desire to be welcomed into heaven in the same way, to have God rush out to meet us when we finally pass from this life into eternal life.

Thanks be to our merciful God, that's just the way it will be. God will welcome us with outstretched arms, with a joy that we cannot even begin to imagine.

God created us out of love and continues to love us passionately. We are God's children because he created us. Through Jesus, we are his adopted sons and daughters, heirs to his kingdom. God wants us to be with him. When we finally arrive in heaven, God will rejoice because his children have come home for good.

Thinking about how much parents can love their children may help us to understand God's love. In the TV movie featuring Oprah Winfrey, *The Women of Brewster Place,* a touching scene makes this point.

A young woman is visiting a single mother who has always lived in the ghetto. Holding a small child in her arms, the mother talks about how she loves her children. She marvels at the great mystery of life in the wonder of giving birth. She fiercely loves the baby in her arms. Despite her material poverty, she gives her children the greatest gift of all—a mother's love.

That gives us a small idea of how much God loves us. He made us in his own image (cf. Gen 1:26ff.); we belong to him (cf. Ps 100:3). God desires passionately for us to be with him always. Jesus' life, death, resurrection and ascension enable us to believe that, if we have been faithful to God, we too shall enjoy eternal happiness with God and one another.

The *Catechism* says of the ascension of Jesus: "Only the one who 'came from the Father' can return to the Father: Christ Jesus (Jn 16:28). 'No one has ascended into heaven but he who descended from heaven, the Son of man' (Jn 3:13; cf. Eph 4:8-10). Left to its own natural powers humanity does not have access to the 'Father's house,' to God's life and happiness. Only Christ can open to man such access that we, his members, might have confidence that we too shall go where he, our Head and our Source, has preceded us" (no. 661).

Reflection:

- Watch a father or mother—or a grandparent—hold a newborn infant in a gentle, passionate, awe-filled embrace. Can you imagine God holding you and loving you in that way?

- We are so aware of our sinfulness and fickleness! Sometimes we may find it hard to believe God can love us as he loves Jesus. Think about the cardinal's vision of the Father and Jesus in heaven. Read the story of the prodigal son in Luke 15. Imagine yourself being forgiven by an earthly father. Imagine yourself—for it will happen through faith and God's mercy—jumping into the Father's embrace when at last you reach home in heaven.

Chapter 9

From Thence He Will Come to Judge the Living and the Dead...

What makes TV shows such as *L.A. Law, The Commish, COPS,* and *NYPD Blue* so popular? Perhaps people are fed up with crime and want to feel more secure and protected. These programs somehow show that good can win over evil—even though a lot of evil is committed by the supposedly good guys. In spite of gory violence and immorality galore, the ultimate message is that right wins over wrong, and this in a small way gives people some hope for security amidst insecurity.

Without profanity, nudity and violence, *Perry Mason, People's Court* and *Murder She Wrote* also capitalize on the public need for justice and good winning over evil. Justice is a desirable commodity in our secular society.

Paradoxically, most of us are not so enthusiastic about the ultimate justice—God's judgment. We do not want to talk about the second coming of Christ and the judgment of the world. People argue timelines and want to believe that "the end" is far off—and it may well be. But rather than face the reality of final judgment and the end of time, many of us get nervous and try to laugh it off or change the subject. We might fear the second coming because of "fire and brimstone" scare tactics in "ole time religion."

On the other hand, we may not fear God at all because some misguided religious personalities and our secular society try to explain away God's supremacy over creation, ignoring his will and commandments. Today many worldly philosophies compete with religion. Hedonistic pursuits and instant gratification of all desires become the norm, regardless of consequences to self and others. For people so misguided, God's commandments are merely "possible suggestions" rather than direction from a loving Father who knows and wants what is best for his children.

Some people have even convinced themselves that heaven and hell are only fairy tales. Or they think that heaven exists but not hell, because a loving God could not possibly create a hell and put people there "just for being human"!

All these distractions, whether willful or unconscious, are rooted in an unhealthy fear of death, of God, of personal accountability for one's actions, and of God's judgment.

The gospel accounts of the second coming do contain some very disturbing prophesies. However, Luke (21:25-36) offers comforting words. After painting a picture of the distressing "signs in the sun, the moon, and the stars," he tells us: "The powers of the heavens will be shaken. Then they will see 'the Son of Man coming in a cloud' with power and great glory. *Now when these things begin to take place, stand up and raise your heads, because your redemption is drawing near*" (emphasis added). The second coming is primarily a salvation event. We have only to reach out to God here and now to be saved for eternal life.

In the fullness of time, Jesus will come again to judge the living and the dead. As the Lord of heaven and earth, Jesus already reigns over the world "through the Church, but all the things of this world are not yet subjected to him. The triumph of Christ's kingdom will not come about without one last assault by the powers of evil.... Christ will come in glory to achieve the definitive triumph of good over evil.... The glorious Christ will reveal the secret disposition of hearts and will render to each man according to his works and according to his acceptance or refusal of grace" *(CCC,* nos. 680-82).

God's justice is even "more just" than what we applaud in movies and TV shows. Christ died so that we might become reconciled with God and live with God forever, in perfect joy and love. Our judge is the God who became a human being and died for us. He is a good and compassionate judge indeed. Human justice can only hint at God's wisdom and compassion. Human justice is true justice only when it is rooted in God's will and wisdom. The path to the wisdom of knowing and accepting God's will is outlined by Mother Teresa:

> The fruit of silence is prayer;
> The fruit of prayer is faith;
> The fruit of faith is love;
> The fruit of love is service;
> The fruit of service is justice;
> The fruit of justice is peace.

God is pure goodness and holiness. The greatest injustice is to take away from God what belongs to him. Satan, the father of sin and lies, has tried to take us away from God. To be just to God is to give ourselves back to him and to help others return to him. The sin of Adam and Eve—and all the sins of all time including our own—separate us from God. The death and resurrection of Jesus defeated Satan and set us free so that Satan can no longer control us. Jesus has swung the doors to the Father's house wide open. All we have to do is to be truly sorry for having offended our good and compassionate Father, confess our sins, change our lives and trust in him. Through Baptism we are now the Body of Christ, members of the Son of God, co-heirs to the kingdom of heaven. Through obedience and grace, we are now back in the Father's house. But the effects of sin still cling to us, so that we have to keep on fighting temptation and evil (cf. nos. 978, 1264, 2520).

Since God loves us, the second coming and the judgment itself should not make us tremble. God knows we are weak and that we sin, and he forgives so easily. If he expects us to forgive one another seventy times seven times (cf. Mt 19:21-22), how much more willing is he to forgive us? The *Catechism's* teaching on the second coming and the judgment is worth our reading and reflection (cf. nos. 668-682).

Christians must not let fear of judgment deter them from trusting in the mercy of God. Rather, the guilt we feel for our misdeeds is an actual grace from God nudging us toward confession and repentance. God does not want to condemn us. Hell is the abode of Satan, and people put themselves there by refusing to accept God's truth, love and mercy. Our great and good God made us for life and joy, not death and suffering.

Reflection:

- When you consider that Jesus "will come again to judge the living and the dead," what comes to mind? How do you react to the prospect of personal judgment?
- Read John 8:1-11. How does Jesus respond to the fear of the sinful woman? To the sinful accusers? What does Jesus ask of the woman and of us?

Chapter 10

I Believe in the Holy Spirit...

A long time ago, an older friend, with a twinkle in his eye, asked me, "Who is the Holy Spirit?" Somewhat puzzled, I promptly replied, "Why, the Holy Spirit is the sanctifier, the comforter, the teacher." Sammy grinned, "That's what he does, but who is he?"

"Well," I said, "he is the Third Person of the Holy Trinity."

Sammy grinned. "Yes, that's true. But who is this Third Person of the Holy Trinity? Tell me about him."

I was stumped. I knew the Holy Spirit only by title.

Sammy left me hanging and I hung there for many years until, after the actual grace called "baptism in the Holy Spirit," I became more aware of the Spirit as a Person and a personal influence in my life and the life of the Church.

The Holy Spirit reveals to us Jesus Christ as Lord (cf. 1 Cor 12:3). The Holy Spirit teaches us that God is such an intimate and loving Father that we can address him with the endearing *Abba!* Father! (cf. Gal 4:6). The *Catechism of the Catholic Church* quotes John (17:3) when it teaches: "Through his grace, the Holy Spirit is the first to awaken faith in us and to communicate to us the new life, which is to 'know the Father and the one whom he has sent, Jesus Christ'" (no. 684).

Through the power of the Spirit we can receive the real Body and Blood of Jesus in Communion. In Eucharistic Prayer I, the priest prays: "Let your Spirit come upon these gifts to make them holy, so that they may become for us the body and blood of our Lord, Jesus Christ." Prayer IV states, "Father, may this Holy Spirit sanctify these offerings. Let them become for us the body and blood of Jesus Christ our Lord."

Since Vatican Council II, Catholics have become more aware of the power and role of the Holy Spirit. However, Catholics have always believed that the Holy Spirit transforms us in Baptism and strengthens us through all the sacraments.

If we experience a deep reverence for God, if we stand in awe of that God who is Three in One, it is by the power of the Holy Spirit. If we love God and one another, we do so because the Holy Spirit teaches and forms us. If we resist temptation, remain faithful to a spouse and refuse to steal, to gossip or to malign or oppress another person, it is because of the Holy Spirit. Likewise, the Spirit gives people the power to do good works and to overcome timidity in sharing faith. When a Christian comforts a bereaved person, advises couples contemplating marriage or helps an unbeliever to believe, the Holy Spirit inspires action and provides the right words, the correct spiritual direction.

If we know that we must love both God and neighbor, it is because of the Spirit; likewise, the Spirit helps us to understand that God loves each one of us with a Father's love. Finally, through the Spirit's powerful gift of wisdom we become fully transformed into the image of Christ.

We receive spiritual strength to do this through the seven gifts of the Spirit received in Baptism and intensified in Confirmation (cf. no. 1831): wisdom, understanding, counsel, fortitude, knowledge, piety and fear of the Lord (or reverence for God).

When we live in the Spirit of God, our lives bear beautiful fruit: "By contrast, the fruit of the Spirit is love, joy, peace, patience, kindness, generosity, faithfulness, gentleness, and self-control. There is no law against such things" (Gal 5:22-23).

As the *Catechism* states so clearly: "The Holy Spirit is at work with the Father and the Son from the beginning to the completion of the plan for our salvation" (no. 686). Only the Spirit understands the thoughts of God (cf. 1 Cor 2:11). "God's Spirit, who reveals God, makes known to us Christ," but "the Spirit does not speak of himself." He "makes us hear the Father's Word.... We know him only in the movement by which he reveals the Word to us and disposes us to welcome him in faith.... Those who believe in Christ know the Spirit because he dwells with them" (no. 687).

Perhaps Christians come to an awareness of the Spirit gradually, just as he came to be known gradually through revelation. The *Catechism* (no. 684) quotes St. Gregory of Nazianzus, fourth century bishop of Constantinople and doctor of the Church:

"The Old Testament proclaimed the Father clearly, but the Son more obscurely. The New Testament revealed the Son and gave us a glimpse of the divinity of the Spirit. Now the Spirit dwells among us and grants us a clearer vision of himself. It was not prudent...when the divinity of the Son was not yet admitted, to add the Holy Spirit as an extra burden, to speak somewhat daringly.... By advancing and progressing 'from glory to glory,' the light of the Trinity will shine in ever more brilliant rays."

So many of the problems facing individuals, families

and society today could be dealt with more effectively through the power of the Holy Spirit. Catholics can benefit greatly by learning more about the Holy Spirit through the wonderful gift of the *Catechism of the Catholic Church*.

As we seek to grow in the grace and life of the Spirit of God, Catholics must remember that the Spirit acts in and through the Church. He is present to us in the Scriptures he inspired, in the Tradition and teachings of the Church, in the liturgy, in prayer, in the signs of apostolic and missionary life and in the witness of the saints (cf. no. 688).

Prayer

Come Holy Spirit, fill the hearts of your faithful and kindle in them the fire of your love. Send forth your Spirit and they shall be created and you shall renew the face of the earth.

Reflection:

- After Jesus' resurrection and ascension, the apostles were filled with fear. But the Holy Spirit came upon them on Pentecost. Prayerfully read chapter two of the Acts of the Apostles—how the Spirit changed the followers of Jesus.

- In what ways does the Spirit manifest himself in our Church today? In your own life?

CHAPTER 11

The Holy Catholic Church...

The zealous Southern Baptist asked the young Catholic, "Are you a Christian or a Catholic?" The Catholic woman hesitated only a moment and replied, "To say I am a Catholic is to say I am a Christian. The Catholic Church was founded by Jesus. I follow Jesus in and through the Catholic Church."

Sometimes other Christians say that Catholics are not Christians, that they put their faith in what St. Paul condemned as "philosophy and empty deceit, according to human tradition" (Col 2:8). They assume that Catholics do not sufficiently respect the Bible, that they "worship" Mary, practice superstition in their sacramental faith and worship idols because they venerate the saints.

But we have to be careful. While the Apostles' Creed states that we believe "in the holy Catholic Church," the *Catechism of the Catholic Church* carefully draws a distinction. We believe in God but we "profess one holy Church" (nos. 750, 169). "Salvation comes from God alone; but because we receive the life of faith through the Church, she is our mother: 'We believe the Church as the mother of our new birth, and not *in* the Church as if she were the author of our salvation.' Because she is our mother, she is also our teacher in the faith" (no. 169).

Perhaps some Catholics have at times contributed to the confusion among non-Catholics by speaking more of the aids to salvation than of the Savior. But the fact remains that to be Catholic is to be Christian, to belong to the Church founded by Jesus on the apostles.

"Church" means different things to different people. Many Evangelical and Protestant churches recognize their own local congregation as a church complete unto itself. While we Catholics love our parishes and celebrate the mystery of salvation in and through the local parish, we believe that "Church" is never complete without our bishops and the successor of Peter, the Pope.

Our faith teaches us that the Church is a *sheepfold*, whose only gate is Christ. The Church is the flock which the shepherd calls to himself, nourishes and protects. Even after his resurrection, Christ continues to nourish and lead his sheep through the human shepherds called into his service (cf. no. 754).

The Church is also a *cultivated field* planted and harvested by God. The "true vine is Christ, who gives life and fruitfulness to the branches, that is, to us, who through the Church remain in Christ, without whom we can do nothing" (no. 755).

The Church is also seen as the *"building* of God." Jesus is the cornerstone of that building and we, the people of God, are the building blocks. The Church is built by the apostles on the foundation of Christ. From that foundation, the Church receives solidity and unity (cf. no. 756).

We know that Christ established the Church because it was the will of the Father that he do so. The Church is part of God's plan for salvation. "This 'family of God' is gradually formed and takes shape during the stages of human history, in keeping with the Father's plan" (no. 759).

Our holy Church was instituted by Christ. In the *Dogmatic Constitution on the Church* Vatican II teaches: "The Lord Jesus inaugurated his Church by preaching the Good News, that is, the coming reign of God, promised over the ages in the Scriptures." That same document also holds: "The Church is the reign of Christ already present in mystery" (nos. 5, 3). The Church, states the *Catechism,* is born of "Christ's total self-giving for our salvation, anticipated in the institution of the Eucharist and fulfilled on the cross" (no. 766).

In the last twenty-five years, Catholics have witnessed a new outpouring of the Holy Spirit. Through liturgical renewal, the Cursillo, Marriage Encounter, the Charismatic Renewal and other movements, we have seen the gifts and fruits of the Holy Spirit poured out anew, enlivening the Church.

Sent on Pentecost, the Holy Spirit continually sanctifies the Church. The Holy Spirit gave the apostles and disciples courage after that first Pentecost to manifest faith and preach the Good News. The Spirit continues to do so through "varied hierarchic and charismatic gifts" (nos. 767-768).

Pope Pius XII gave us the encyclical which calls the Church the Mystical Body of Christ. As the Body of Christ, the Church is both human and divine, "visible but endowed with invisible realities, zealous in action and dedicated to contemplation, present in the world, but as a pilgrim, so constituted that in her the human is directed toward and subordinated to the divine, the visible to the invisible, action to contemplation, and this present world to that city yet to come, the object of our quest" (no. 771).

So much more can be said of the Church. The *Catechism of the Catholic Church* is a wonderful treasure for Catholics who want to know more about their faith. We come to know and love God through the Church. To know and practice our Catholic faith well is to enter into the mercy, love and wisdom of God.

In the next chapter we will continue this review of the Church.

Reflection:

- In what ways do we sometimes contribute to other Christians' wrong impressions about what we believe and in whom we place our faith?
- Find a Catholic whose spirituality differs from yours. Share together why you both practice your faith as you do.
- Reflect on that sharing in light of the content in this chapter.

CHAPTER 12

The Holy Catholic Church... *(continued)*

Older Catholics will remember the response to the *Baltimore Catechism* question: "What is a sacrament?" The answer: "A sacrament is an outward sign of inward grace." Older Catholics who were asked for the definition of sanctifying grace responded, "It is a gift from God!" Thank goodness no one asked us to explain that!

When I was a young adult, I taught a CCD class of high-school girls. I had learned that sanctifying grace was, in one definition, "a share in the divine life of God." I was bent on helping them to amplify the rote answer, "Sanctifying grace is a gift from God." For weeks, I talked about how sanctifying grace was a share in the very life of God. At the end of the semester, I conducted an oral quiz. "What is sanctifying grace?" I asked.

"It is a gift from God," they all replied in unison.

Undaunted, I asked, "And what is that gift from God?"

After a pause, one girl asked hesitantly, "Sanctifying grace?"

Well, you lose some and you lose some.

I was just as puzzled when theologians began talking about the Church as a sacrament. After all, Mama and the *Baltimore Catechism* said there were only seven sacraments.

Thank God for the new *Catechism of the Catholic Church*. The consideration of the Church as a kind of sacrament becomes clearer:

"Christ himself is the mystery of salvation: 'For there is no other mystery of God, except Christ.' The saving work of his holy and sanctifying humanity is the sacrament of salvation, which is revealed and active in the Church's sacraments.... The seven sacraments are the signs and instruments by which the Holy Spirit spreads the grace of Christ the head throughout the Church which is his Body. The Church, then, both contains and communicates the invisible grace she signifies. It is in this analogical sense that the Church is called a 'sacrament.'"

Going back to the traditional definition of sacrament given above: "A sacrament is an outward sign of inward grace," the Church is (analogically) an outward sign of God's presence and sanctifying action in the world, containing within itself the graces of all the sacraments. The Church is a mystery because it is the people of God, a community of believing people, who are the recipients and the sign of the Father's gifts given in Christ through the Spirit.

"The Church, in Christ, is like a sacrament—a sign and instrument, that is, of communion with God and of unity among men." The Church's first purpose is to be the sacrament of the *inner union of men with God.* Because men's communion with one another is rooted in that union with God, the Church is also the sacrament of the *unity of the human race.* In her this unity is already begun, since she gathers men 'from every nation, from all tribes and peoples and tongues'; at the same time, the Church is the "sign and instrument" of the full realization of the unity yet to come (nos. 774-775).

The Holy Catholic Church... *(continued)*

The Church is also called the People of God. The Church is not bricks and cement, but flesh and blood and spirit. "The Church" means those who profess and belong to the one, holy, catholic and apostolic Church. God accepts all people who fear him and do what is right. But God has decided "to make people holy and to save them, not as individuals without any bond or link between them, but rather to make them into a people who might acknowledge him and serve him in holiness" (*Lumen Gentium*, no. 9). He chose the Israelites, and he has chosen the people of the New Covenant formed in the Blood of Christ *(Catechism,* no. 781).

As Church, we are God's people. We belong to him; he is not our property. We become members of the People of God by being reborn of water and the Spirit. Jesus the Christ (the Anointed) is the head of his people, of his Body, the Church. The anointing of the Spirit flows from the Head to the entire Body to make of them the "messianic people." As God's people, as members of the Church, we are given the dignity and freedom of sons and daughters of God, with the Holy Spirit dwelling in our hearts. Our law is the commandment of Christ to love one another. Our mission is to be the salt of the earth and the light of the world. We are the seed of unity, hope and salvation sown by God in the field of the world. Our destiny is the kingdom of God, "which has been begun by God himself on earth and which must be further extended until it has been brought to perfection by him at the end of time" (no. 782).

Using the *Catechism* as a resource for prayer and reflection, we can all learn more about ourselves and other believing Christians who form the Church founded by Jesus Christ. We can study and reflect on what it means to be a priestly, prophetic and royal people of God. We can pursue greater holiness in the Church, which is a communion with Jesus. We can try to understand better what it means to be one Body with Christ as its Head, what it means to be the bride of Christ, the temple of the Holy Spirit, and to receive, enjoy and use the charisms of the Spirit.

To be Christian is to enter the kingdom of God. To be Catholic is to enjoy the fullness of revelation and the means of salvation and holiness.

Reflection:

- What has "church" meant to you? A place to go? The Pope, bishops, priests and nuns? Or what?
- How has your understanding and definition of "church" changed over the years?
- In your own words, tell a friend what it means to say the Church is a "sacrament."

Chapter 13

The Communion of Saints...

My father was nearly ninety-five when he died. As a deacon, I presided at the wake, remembering Dad's great sense of hospitality. Father Joe, the pastor in our family's rural Louisiana parish, preached the homily at the Mass of Christian Burial. He spoke of Dad's stately bearing. Father Joe said that this man—who had worked hard as a farmer, carpenter and laborer—walked like a king. Even at such an advanced age, he was straight and he looked people in the eye.

Father Joe's words consoled us greatly. Our father had indeed been a good man, a good husband and father. He had been a good Catholic and citizen, a soldier in World War I. But the real consolation came when Father Joe reminded us that Dad and Mom and all our relatives could live together forever with God, that all who remain faithful would be with them again some day. Even though they were now in eternity, we were not separated from them. We are with them in prayer, in communion with God.

That's what our Church teaches. The saints are always in touch with God and with one another. Even death cannot separate us from those who have gone before us. They are with God and we are too, so together we are with

God. This communion is a spiritual bonding, a spiritual "touching" and "talking" and "embracing."

As the *Catechism of the Catholic Church* explains: "The communion of saints is the Church," and the most important member of that communion is Christ, who is the Head of the Body (nos. 946, 947). The Church has three states—some of us are pilgrims on earth; some have died and are being purified; still others are in glory and see our Triune God as he is (cf. no. 954).

As saints who make up the Church under Jesus Christ, we have a *communion of faith*. Our faith comes to us from the apostles and is "a treasure of life which is enriched by being shared." We have *communion in the sacraments*, which unite the faithful to one another and bind them to Jesus Christ. Baptism is the "gate by which we enter into the Church." *Communion* happens in and through all the sacraments, but the name *Communion* "is better suited to the Eucharist than to any other, because it is primarily the Eucharist that brings this communion about" (nos. 949-950).

We also experience *communion in charisms* (gifts of the Holy Spirit). The Holy Spirit dispenses his various gifts to different people, all for enriching the Church. Who could forget the outstanding preaching of Bishop Sheen, the charity of Mother Teresa, the simplicity of St. Francis, the zeal for truth of St. Paul and Pope John Paul II? Bishop Sheen and Mother Teresa are two great examples of how individual gifts from God build up the Body of Christ and inspire the world. Protestants as well as Catholics listened to Bishop Sheen. Even non-believers were captivated by his clarity of thought, zeal and humor. Mother Teresa is perhaps, like St. Francis, one of the Church's great counter-cultural signs. She has touched the hearts of people throughout the world. With the gifts of the Holy

Spirit, even the most ordinary Christian mother, father, carpenter, physician or laborer builds up the Church when serving out of love and adhering to the truths and disciplines of the Gospel and the Church (cf. no. 951).

We are also enriched by our *communion in charity*. Even the least of all acts done out of love benefits the entire body, for what benefits one, benefits all, and what hurts one hurts all. That love leads Christians to share their material and spiritual blessings with others: "Everything the true Christian has is to be regarded as a good possessed in common with everyone else. All Christians should be ready and eager to come to the help of the needy...and of their neighbors in want." A Christian is the steward of the Lord's goods (nos. 952-953).

We are blessed with another benefit from the communion of saints: the prayers of saints in heaven enrich the Church in the world. These saints, who are with God in eternity, continue to intercede for us. Their loving concern and prayers help us in our weakness. When St. Dominic was dying, he said to his brothers: "Do not weep, for I shall be more useful to you after my death and I shall help you then more effectively than during my life." St. Therese of Lisieux wrote, "I want to spend my heaven doing good on earth" (no. 956).

In this beautiful communion of saints, God is our Father, Christ is our Lord, Savior and Brother, and the Holy Spirit is our Advocate, Teacher and Comforter. And we are all brothers and sisters. But that is not all. God has given us a mother, Mary, the mother of Jesus. The *Catechism* teaches that Mary is "the Mother of God and of the redeemer... She is 'clearly the mother of the members of Christ'...since she has by her charity joined in bringing about the birth of believers in the Church, who are members of its head" (no. 963).

Mary's union with Christ extended from the moment of his conception throughout his entire life, even to his death. She shared in "her mother's heart" the suffering of Jesus and willingly gave her Son as the victim of sacrifice for the salvation of the world. After Christ's ascension, Mary was present with the disciples at Pentecost and she "aided the beginnings of the young Church by her prayers" (nos. 964-965).

Because of her obedience to God and her fidelity to God's will, she is our model of faith and charity. "In a wholly singular way, she cooperated by her obedience, faith, hope and burning charity in the Savior's work of restoring supernatural life to souls. For this reason she is a mother to us in the order of grace" (nos. 967-968).

Reflection:

- Do you sometimes feel as though a deceased loved one is near? Or do you sometimes ask a deceased friend or relative to pray for you?
- Is the "communion of saints" a doctrine that gives you a special place and responsibility in the Church?
- The next time you pray or receive Communion, try to be more aware of how you are in the presence of all the saints and of God.

CHAPTER 14

The Forgiveness of Sins...

Not seeing the old man sitting in the back of the church, the girl walked directly to the life-sized crucifix in the sanctuary. She knelt before the crucified one, then rose and hugged the foot of the cross, looking up at the image of Jesus. "I love you, Jesus," she said over and over again. "I love you Jesus. I love you Jesus...."

The old man slipped silently to his knees, feeling his sinfulness weigh on him. He was so moved by the girl's love for God, that he felt as though he were an intruder, an outsider. Yet the scene in the sanctuary filled him with a warmth he had never before known. He felt as though someone were embracing him. He felt the loving presence of God.

The old man was like the publican in the gospel story who stayed in the back of the synagogue, striking his breast, telling God he was sinful and unworthy of God's love (cf. Lk 18:9-14). The sight of the young woman loving God so openly and with such abandon moved him to see himself in a new light and helped him realize the beauty of God's love. Through the girl's faith, he became open to God's love. The "Hound of Heaven" finally caught him.

In recent years, the trend has been to treat the pain of guilt rather than the cause of guilt. Guilt can become excessive and even pathological, but guilt can be healthy, a normal emotion which lets us know we have done something wrong, something against God's will. As Catholics, we cannot take a mere psychological approach to guilt, but must consider guilt as a result of sin. Sometimes, when people are not sensitive to the commandments and the teachings of the Church, or when they have not formed a good conscience, they have no conscious experience of guilt. That makes sorrow for sin and the desire to change one's life all but impossible.

God's commandments are not imposed from above in an oppressive spirit. Rather, God's commandments and the teachings of the Church are given to help us become all we can become, to discover true freedom which is found only in doing God's will. (Read Pope John Paul II's *Splendor of Truth.*)

As Catholics, we seek forgiveness in the Sacrament of Reconciliation. In this beautiful sacrament, the sinner finds forgiveness from God and reconciliation with God and the Church. Even private sin affects the entire Church, since what affects one part of the body affects the entire body.

In the *Catechism of the Catholic Church,* we read:

"The Creed links 'the forgiveness of sins' with its profession of faith in the Holy Spirit, for the risen Christ entrusted to the apostles the power to forgive sins when he gave them the Holy Spirit" (no. 984).

"By Christ's will, the Church possesses the power to forgive the sins of the baptized and exercises it through bishops and priests normally in the Sacrament of Penance [Reconciliation].

"In the forgiveness of sins, both priests and sacraments are instruments which our Lord Jesus Christ, the only author and liberal giver of salvation, wills to use in order to efface our sins and give us the grace of justification" (nos. 986-987).

Furthermore, the *Catechism* (no. 1442) holds that "Christ...entrusted the exercise of the power of absolution to the apostolic ministry which he charged with the 'ministry of reconciliation'" (2 Cor 5:18).

And, in "imparting to his apostles his own power to forgive sins the Lord also gives them the authority to reconcile sinners with the Church. This ecclesial dimension of their task is expressed most notably in Christ's solemn words to Simon Peter: 'I will give you the keys of the kingdom of heaven, and whatever you bind on earth shall be bound in heaven, and whatever you loose on earth shall be loosed in heaven'" (no. 1444, quoting Mt 16:19, cf. Mt 18:18; 28:16-20). Vatican II's *Lumen Gentium* teaches that the "office of binding and loosing which was given to Peter was also assigned to the college of the apostles united to its head." The power to forgive sins is passed on to bishops by the sacrament of Holy Orders in the laying on of hands.

The *Catechism* further explains, "The words *bind and loose* mean: whomever you exclude from your communion, will be excluded from communion with God; whomever you receive anew into your communion, God will welcome back into his. *Reconciliation with the Church is inseparable from reconciliation with God"* (no. 1445).

The Sacrament of Reconciliation (also called Penance or Confession) was given to us by Christ for all sinful members of the Church, especially those guilty of grave sin after having been baptized. For a thorough review of the great sacrament, readers may consult the *Catechism of the Catholic Church,* numbers 1422-1470. However, given the modern timidity which accompanies the thought of telling another human being one's sins, we should emphasize the following teaching from the *Catechism:*

"Confession to a priest is an essential part of the Sacrament of Penance: 'All mortal sins of which penitents after a diligent self-examination are conscious must be recounted by them in confession, even if they are most secret and have been committed against the last two precepts of the Decalogue [the ten commandments, the last two of which tell us not to covet our neighbor's wife or goods]; for these sins sometimes wound the soul more grievously and are more dangerous than those which are committed openly" (no. 1456).

The Church tells us we must confess our serious sins at least once a year. While it is not necessary to confess venial sins (daily faults), the Church "strongly recommends" that we do so. "The regular confession of venial sins helps us form our conscience, fight against evil tendencies, let ourselves be healed by Christ and progress in the life of the Spirit" (no. 1458).

Finally, it is hard to be open to God's forgiveness if we do not forgive others. This story underscores that point.

An angry, tearful woman confronted a priest who had preached on forgiveness. The priest had said that Christians had no choice but to forgive if they were to be faithful to the Gospel.

The woman had been physically and emotionally abused by her ex-husband. She was truly a battered woman. Sobbing, she told the priest: "I can't forgive him. I didn't deserve what he did to me and if I forgive him, I'm admitting that he was right in abusing me!"

The woman later admitted she had never felt forgiven for her own sins. Her resentment, anger and unforgiveness had made her miserable. The priest explained to her that forgiving her ex-husband did not mean he was right in abusing her: "Jesus forgave. He offered his suffering for the salvation of us all—including the people who nailed him to the cross. His act of forgiveness did not make him deserve the injustice of the cross. If you forgive the man who hurt you, you are not saying you deserved the abuse. Forgiving an offender releases us from the prison of resentment and opens us to God's forgiveness."

The woman learned gradually to forgive, and as she forgave, she became happier until she was finally free from resentment. She still remembers the pain and is saddened by the memory, but she is no longer a prisoner of bitterness. She is free of unhealthy guilt and knows she is forgiven for her own sins.

The Lord Jesus was both prophet and teacher when he taught us to pray, "Forgive us our trespasses as we forgive those who trespass against us."

Reflection:

- St. Paul said that Jesus died for us while we were still sinners (cf. Rom 5:8). That meant he loves us when we are at our worst. Do you believe this? If so, what is your response to such unconditional love?

- If there is still someone whom you have not forgiven, do so now! Just pray: "Lord Jesus, I'm still hurt. I don't feel like forgiving that person, but I decide to do so, in spite of my feelings! You forgive me, Jesus. I must forgive others."

CHAPTER 15

The Resurrection of the Body...

In the movies *Ghost* and *Always,* a principal character dies and in one way or another remains involved with the lives of people still on earth. Both movies at best give a brief and hesitant nod to the Christian belief in life after death.

As Christians, we do not see death as the end of life, but as a transition to a more glorious and everlasting life. We do not believe in reincarnation, as do some non-Christian religions and neo-philosophies such as the New Age movement. We believe that God created each of us individually and we are destined to live for all eternity. We believe that at death, our souls leave our bodies which, in turn, suffer corruption, but on the last day our mortal bodies will be raised from the dead. They will be spiritual bodies, glorified with and in Christ, but they will be our own bodies.

The *Catechism of the Catholic Church* has a beautiful section on death, resurrection and life everlasting. Catholics, and all believers, can benefit from reading and reflecting on the truths presented there. Here is a sampling of the teachings on death, resurrection and everlasting life found in the *Catechism* (nos. 988-1065).

• God created human beings as a substantial union of body and soul; the Son of God, the Second Person of the Blessed Trinity, became a man (Jesus of Nazareth) who was completely human with a body of flesh and a human soul. Jesus' death redeemed humanity from sin and made it possible for people to return to the Father.

• Jesus rose from the dead. He is called the first fruits of the dead, meaning that others will also rise from the dead. At the end of the world, all the dead will rise: some to glory in Christ Jesus, the unfaithful and evil ones to an eternity without God.

• "God revealed the resurrection of the dead to his people progressively...." The Pharisees and many of the Lord's contemporaries hoped for the resurrection. Jesus teaches it firmly" (nos. 992-993). St. Augustine said that resurrection of the dead was the most opposed point of Christian faith. People may have believed in the soul's living forever, but not in the rising of a body that had been returned to dust.

• What is rising and how will it be accomplished? The body will be raised by the Holy Trinity, who raised Jesus from the dead. It will be given incorruptibility and glorified in Christ's own glory. Jesus rose from the dead in his real body. He said, "See my hands and my feet." He told Thomas to put his fingers into the nail prints in his hands and into his wounded side. The *Catechism* teaches (quoting the Lateran Council, Philippians and 1 Corinthians): "So, in him, [Jesus Christ] 'all of them will rise again with their own bodies which they now bear' but Christ 'will change our lowly body to be like his glorious body,' into 'a spiritual body'" (no. 999).

We can't even begin to imagine "how" God will accomplish our own personal resurrection, but we believe it in faith. Our faith tells us we already have a foretaste of our resurrection because we participate in the Eucharist. The *Catechism* quotes St. Irenaeus: "Just as bread that comes from the earth, after God's blessing has been invoked upon it, is no longer bread, but Eucharist, formed of two things, the one earthly and the other heavenly: so too our bodies, which partake of the Eucharist, are no longer corruptible, but possess the hope of resurrection" (no. 1000).

Through the sacraments, we are taught, we already have died and risen in Christ. As the Apostle Paul tells us in Colossians (2:12, 3:1): "When you were buried with him in baptism, you were also raised with him through faith in the power of God, who raised him from the dead.... So if you have been raised with Christ, seek the things that are above, where Christ is, seated at the right hand of God."

In faith we joyfully await that day when we will see God face to face, and that day when our bodies will be resurrected and reunited to our souls. Our joyful and expectant faith, through our sacramental spirituality and in communion with all the saints, enables us to participate even now, however imperfectly, in that resurrection and everlasting life which is in Christ Jesus.

Reflection:

- Sometimes people try to ignore the reality of death. Could it be because they do not believe in eternal life? Are people drawn to fictional accounts of "ghosts" because somehow, deep inside, they want to live forever?

- Have you ever had a "resurrection experience" such as recovering from a serious illness or finding hope after a time of anxiety or even despair?

- Spend some quiet time thinking of how you, made in God's image, will live forever. Thank God for your own eternal life—body and soul.

Chapter 16

And Life Everlasting...

The most difficult duty I've ever performed as a deacon was presiding and preaching at a wake service for a sixteen-year-old boy who had died of cancer. He had been such a courageous person. Many high school students attended the wake. Some were weeping; all seemed stunned, bewildered as they faced the reality that even the young die. The great unasked, unanswered and unanswerable question was: "Why?"

As I faced the parents and young brothers and sisters of the deceased, as I saw his grieving friends, I realized anew the importance of our Catholic faith, of our belief in everlasting life, and how difficult it is in today's world to have faith. But we do have faith, a free gift in Baptism, a faith that is nourished and strengthened through all the sacraments, through our private prayers and community worship at the Eucharist.

A dear friend frequently reminds me: "God does not lie. If God says there is everlasting life, there is everlasting life." That, I believe, is the foundation of our faith: God does not lie. God keeps his promises.

Our hearts sing with joy as we hear again and again the great truth in those familiar words: "Whoever believes in me shall have life everlasting" (cf. Jn 6:47).

"Those who eat my flesh and drink my blood have eternal life, and I will raise them up on the last day" (Jn 6:54).

"I am the way, and the truth, and the life" (Jn 14:6).

The *Catechism of the Catholic Church* (nos. 1020-1060) presents an organized and easy-to-read teaching on everlasting life, heaven, purgatory, hell and judgment. An overview of that teaching follows.

The Christian who unites his or her death to that of Jesus takes a step toward Jesus and eternal life. Death itself is the end of a person's opportunity to make decisions about life, morality, and the most weighty of all choices: acceptance of Jesus Christ as Lord of life and Savior, as the way, the truth and the life, as the only way to the Father.

We will all receive eternal reward or punishment for our choices on earth. In the "particular judgment," our lives are measured against that of Christ, his teachings and the call and commandments of God. The soul goes "either into the blessedness of heaven—through a purification or immediately—or [the soul goes to] immediate and everlasting damnation" (no. 1022).

The *Catechism* describes heaven, hell and purgatory.

Heaven

"Those who die in God's grace and friendship and are perfectly purified live for ever with Christ. They are like God for ever, for they 'see him as he is,' face to face" (cf. 1 Jn 3:2, 1 Cor 13:12 and Rev 22:4).... This perfect life with the Most Holy Trinity—this communion of life and love with the Trinity, with the Virgin Mary, the angels and all the blessed—is called 'heaven'" (nos. 1023-1024). In heaven we become fully what God intended us to be, perfected, sinless, without sorrow or suffering.

The death and resurrection of Jesus Christ opened heaven to us. Heavenly happiness "consists in the full and perfect possession of the fruits of the redemption accomplished by Christ. He makes partners in his heavenly glorification those who have believed in him and remained faithful to his will." As St. Cyprian said, "How great will your glory and happiness be, to be allowed to see God, to be honored with sharing the joy of salvation and eternal light with Christ your Lord and God...to delight in the joy of immortality in the kingdom of heaven with the righteous and God's friends" (nos. 1026-1028).

Purgatory

"All who die in God's grace and friendship, but still imperfectly purified, are indeed assured of their eternal salvation; but after death they undergo purification, so as to achieve the holiness necessary to enter the joy of heaven" (no. 1030).

The Church calls this final purification "purgatory." This final purification is entirely different from the punishment of the damned. The doctrine of purgatory was defined at the Councils of Florence and Trent, based on the tradition of the Church which speaks of "cleansing fire" and on certain Scripture passages. St. Gregory the Great notes the text about the unforgivable sin of blasphemy against the Holy Spirit. He says the Scripture states that such a sin "will be pardoned neither in this age nor in the age to come." St. Gregory concludes, "From this sentence we can understand that certain offenses can be forgiven in this age, but certain others in the age to come." In 2 Maccabees 12:46 we read: "Therefore [Judas Maccabeus] made atonement for the dead, that they might be delivered from their sin." From the beginning, long before schisms and protestations, the Church "honored the memory of the dead and offered prayers in suffrage for them, above all the Eucharistic sacrifice, so that, thus purified, they may attain the beatific vision of God" (Council of Lyons). "The Church also commends almsgiving, indulgences, and works of penance undertaken on behalf of the dead..." (nos. 1030-1032).

Hell

No one can be united with God except by freely choosing to love him. To love God is to listen to him, to obey him, to do his will. But we cannot love God if we sin gravely against him, against our neighbor or against ourselves. "Whoever does not love abides in death. All who hate a brother or sister are murderers, and you know that murderers do not have eternal life abiding in them" (1 Jn 3:14-15).

The Church defines "hell" as a state of definitive self-exclusion from communion with God and the blessed. This self-exclusion could occur when a seriously sinful person dies without repenting and accepting God's merciful love. Such a death means remaining separated from God forever.

The Church "affirms the existence of hell and its eternity. Immediately after death the souls of those who die in a state of mortal sin descend into hell, where they suffer the punishments of hell.... The chief punishment of hell is eternal separation from God, in whom alone man can possess the life and happiness for which he was created and for which he longs."

God does not send anyone to hell. People choose hell on their own by refusing to come to know, love and serve God. In 2 Peter 3:9, we hear clearly that God does not want "any to perish, but all to come to repentance" (cf. *Catechism,* nos. 1033-1037).

The Last Judgment

All the dead will rise before the final and general judgment. "In the presence of Christ, who is Truth itself, the truth of each man's relationship with God will be laid bare. The last judgment will reveal even to its furthest consequences the good each person has done or failed to do during his earthly life" (1038-1039).

The last judgment will come when Christ returns in glory. Only the Father knows when it will occur. "The Last Judgment will reveal that God's justice triumphs over all the injustices committed by his creatures and that God's love is stronger than death." We look forward to the Lord's Second Coming with a blessed hope to see him "glorified in his saints and to be marveled at in all who have believed" (nos. 1040-1041).

The entire universe will be transformed at the Second Coming. All things will be put in order. Vatican Council II teaches in *Lumen Gentium* that at the Second Coming, "together with the human race, the universe itself, which is so closely related to man and which attains its destiny through him, will be perfectly reestablished in Christ" (no. 1042).

Now, in the light of such a great promise, who on earth could possibly not shout: "Alleluia!"

Reflection:

- Visit a cemetery. Look at all the headstones, the names, dates of birth and death. What happened to all these lives? Were they merely snuffed out like candles? How can a human being—made in God's image—cease to be?

- Over the years, has your understanding changed regarding heaven, hell and purgatory? How has it changed? Compare your present understanding with the teachings of the Church.
- On the feasts of All Saints and All Souls, make a special effort to think seriously about your own future in eternity—and thank God for eternal life.

Chapter 17

Amen!

When I was a fledgling Catholic journalist in the Lafayette, Louisiana Diocese, my editor, Father Alexander O. Sigur, asked me to stand in for him at the dedication of a parsonage. Each clergyman from a visiting church would be asked to say a few words and Father wanted me to do that for him.

I was too young to hesitate, so I said yes. I was too triumphant and uninformed to know that these people of the AME church were truly Christians who knew and loved Jesus Christ. I decided to help them see their spiritual poverty by suggesting, not too subtly, that they did not really know God.

I selected as my Scripture that section from Acts in which Paul confronts the Athenians with the Gospel. He mentions their "altar to the Unknown God" (Acts 17:23) and he proceeds to tell them that their Unknown God is really the God of Abraham, Isaac and Jacob and that his only Son, Jesus Christ, came to redeem them all.

Well, Lordy! I didn't get past reading the Scripture before that church was filled with "Amen!" and "Amen!" and "Preach, brother, preach!"

This shocked my Catholic sensitivity to worship protocol. I forgot what I was going to say and somehow got through it by saying something like "no matter how much we know God and believe in him, we can never know him fully and our faith is never adequate because he is so big and we are so small."

The congregation's unashamed and unintimidated enthusiasm for the Word of God stunned me. Somehow, their "Amens!" said more than what I had to say.

Amen! It is initially surprising to see the *Catechism of the Catholic Church* devoting a small section (nos. 1061–1065) to "Amen," but then we discover good reasons for this. The literal translation of "Amen" from the Hebrew is "it is true" or "yes." It expresses acceptance of what has been said. At the end of formal church prayers, we say, "Amen," that is, we believe in what we have asked, in what we have professed. We believe that God is, that he loves us and hears our prayers. We believe in our communion of faith. We believe in the power of prayer. We have to mean our "Amens!"

We Catholics receive the Body and Blood of Jesus at Mass. The priest holds up the host and says, "The Body of Christ," and with the cup, "The Blood of Christ." We respond, "Amen!" Do we consciously put our heart and soul into that act of faith?

We don't have to shout "Amen!" but we have to mean what we are saying. We are saying, "Yes, I believe this is Jesus Christ, true God and true man, coming to me as food. This is no longer bread and wine, but my Lord and my God."

When we say "Amen!" at the end of the Creed, we are repeating the first words of the Creed, "I believe." At the beginning we profess belief in what we are about to profess. At the end, we reaffirm that belief and acceptance of the tenets of our holy faith.

The *Catechism* reminds us that the Creed, like the last book of the Bible (Revelation), ends with the Hebrew word "Amen." The Church likewise ends her prayers with "Amen."

Isaiah speaks of the "God of truth," which literally translated means the "God of Amen," that is the God who is faithful to his promises.

To say "Amen" at the end of the Creed, the Catechism teaches, is to say "yes" or "I believe." It is "to entrust oneself completely to him who is the 'Amen' of infinite love and perfect faithfulness," Jesus Christ, the Lord. To say "Amen" to truth and love, St. Augustine wrote, is to have the Creed as a mirror. "Look at yourself in it, to see if you believe everything you say you believe. And rejoice in your faith each day."

The *Catechism* concludes this section of the Creed with the following:

"Jesus Christ himself is the 'Amen' (Rev. 3:14). He is the definitive 'Amen' of the Father's love for us. He takes up and completes our 'Amen' to the Father: 'For all the promises of God find their Yes in him. That is why we utter the Amen through him, to the glory of God'" (no. 1065).

Through him, with him, in him,
in the unity of the Holy Spirit,
all glory and honor is yours,
almighty Father,
God, for ever and ever.
AMEN.

Our "Amen" to God must lead to a holy life. Our Church is sacramental. We not only have the Scriptures but the presence and saving action of Jesus Christ in all seven sacraments. The Most Holy Trinity touches us and transforms us by grace through the sacraments. AMEN!

Reflection:

- Indeed! AMEN!

Books by Henry Libersat

Pauline Books & Media

Way, Truth and Life
Do Whatever He Tells You
A Catholic Confession of Faith
   Book One: *We Believe*
   Book Two: *We Celebrate the Mystery*
   Book Three: *We Live the Good Life*
   Book Four: *We Pray*

Servant Publications

Miracles Do Happen
(co-author for Sister Briege McKenna)

Godparents

Rekindle Your Life in the Spirit
(co-author with Babsie Bleasdell)

Pauline BOOKS & MEDIA

ALASKA
  750 West 5th Ave., Anchorage, AK 99501; 907-272-8183
CALIFORNIA
  3908 Sepulveda Blvd., Culver City, CA 90230; 310-397-8676
  5945 Balboa Ave., San Diego, CA 92111; 619-565-9181
  46 Geary Street, San Francisco, CA 94108; 415-781-5180
FLORIDA
  145 S.W. 107th Ave., Miami, FL 33174; 305-559-6715
HAWAII
  1143 Bishop Street, Honolulu, HI 96813; 808-521-2731
ILLINOIS
  172 North Michigan Ave., Chicago, IL 60601; 312-346-4228
LOUISIANA
  4403 Veterans Memorial Blvd., Metairie, LA 70006; 504-887-7631
MASSACHUSETTS
  50 St. Paul's Ave., Jamaica Plain, Boston, MA 02130; 617-522-8911
  Rte. 1, 885 Providence Hwy., Dedham, MA 02026; 617-326-5385
MISSOURI
  9804 Watson Rd., St. Louis, MO 63126; 314-965-3512
NEW JERSEY
  561 U.S. Route 1, Wick Plaza, Edison, NJ 08817; 908-572-1200
NEW YORK
  150 East 52nd Street, New York, NY 10022; 212-754-1110
  78 Fort Place, Staten Island, NY 10301; 718-447-5071
OHIO
  2105 Ontario Street, Cleveland, OH 44115; 216-621-9427
PENNSYLVANIA
  9171-A Roosevelt Blvd., Philadelphia, PA
  19114; 215-676-9494
SOUTH CAROLINA
  243 King Street, Charleston, SC 29401; 803-577-0175
TENNESSEE
  4811 Poplar Ave., Memphis, TN 38117; 901-761-2987
TEXAS
  114 Main Plaza, San Antonio, TX 78205; 210-224-8101
VIRGINIA
  1025 King Street, Alexandria, VA 22314; 703-549-3806
CANADA
  3022 Dufferin Street, Toronto, Ontario, Canada M6B 3T5; 416-781-9131
  1155 Yonge Street, Toronto, Ontario, Canada M4T 1W2; 416-934-3440